Bringing
CEREMONY HOME

Creating Ceremony in an easy at-home format for Spiritual DIYers!

A guide to using The Sacred Circle in normal everyday life situations to facilitate change.

DEANNA KING

5DPath Publishing

Bringing Ceremony Home: Creating Ceremony in an Easy at-Home Format for Spiritual DIYers!
By Deanna King

Published by 5DPath Publishing
Dolores, Colorado, USA

www.5DPath.fun

Contact publisher for bulk orders and permission requests.

Cover concept by Tamara Tyson for **3 ferns books** ➺—➤ www.3fernsbooks.com

Cover and interior book design & formatting
by Leesa Ellis of **3 ferns books** ➺—➤ www.3fernsbooks.com

Printed in the United States of America.

Library of Congress Control Number: 2023908250

ISBN (Hardcover):   979-8-9882869-0-5
ISBN (Paperback):   979-8-9882869-1-2
ISBN (eBook):   979-8-9882869-2-9

TABLE OF CONTENTS

DEDICATION

For all of you Valiant Souls
that chose to come and assist
in this Miraculous "Ascension
of Earth/Gaia and all her
inhabitants."

I Salute You!
Be the Love and the Light
that you are.

Acknowledgements

This book is made possible because of the "**Masterfully Choreographed**" astrological transits that my soul chose to be born within. Starting with my parents, who shaped me and challenged me in ways that I am yet to fully understand. Thank you to my mother, who was a soul beyond her years, and who inspired me and shaped me by osmosis. I acknowledge all the people in my life who have used the spoken word to touch the heart, which will forever be my chosen language. A big thank you to my **Spirit Guides** who have never given up on me, no matter how frustrated I was with their convoluted communication. I acknowledge and thank the myriad of teachers who have nudged me on this soul journey: the shamans, the healers, the friends, the students, the clients, the partners, the podcasts and audios, the astrologers, and the metaphysicians. There are too many beautiful catalysts to name.

A big hug and **thank you** for **all** the people who believe in me and let me know it... Laurie B., Sarah C., Annie T., Reed K., Jaquie B., Jessie F., Jon K., Valencia V., Nicole F., and Mary R.

Stay Magical

To receive your
complimentary
Book Bonuses, visit:

www.bit.ly/BCHBonuses

PREFACE

Who am I to write about Ceremony?

My earliest memories contain a visceral yearning for a connection to an authentic ancestral heritage, or frankly **any** heritage, which would offer some definition to me as an individual in this world. What I knew in my being was that I did not align with my birth family's beliefs, and I certainly did not want to follow the path they were laying out for me. Although now as a wiser adult, I realize my soul had chosen to be born American and experience the freedom of individualism; however, my upbringing did not foster a strong sense of self or individualism. This feeling of **alienation** from my birth family's beliefs perpetuated a sense of loss, **a void in me** to fill. As a female being raised not only in a patriarchal religion, but also a patriarchal community, city, and state, I quickly learned the opposite was true for freedom and individualism. Following the "**American dream**" was never a path that I felt was open to me. Thus, I found the school's curriculum of United States history teachings also confusing to me as a young and vulnerable mind, for the freedom teachings did not align with the religious teachings of my family. In the religion I was raised in, the power went only to the males, and only the males had a direct connection to God. My role was to essentially be a man's servant, loyal and happy of course, but nonetheless a servant, a passive female meant to take direction and guidance from him as well as follow his ideas. Even a child could see through the embellished and exaggerated disempowered role laid out for me. As a female born with an innate strong sense of will and inner drive to be a leader, I became squashed and with no outlet; therefore, of course, I found myself depressed at a young age because of the foreboding hopelessness of the situation. I was taught to completely deny my individualism. I was never shown that I could have a personal and true spiritual connection with God/Source, or become a strong leader of any sort. Unless, of course, I wanted to lead the sewing class, which was not only demeaning but truly uninspiring and wrong in every way for me.

From childhood to my twenties, my early religious formatting and programming had been my primary "taught" spiritual foundation. Even though it felt wrong and did not empower me, it was all I had and knew intimately. Thankfully, my parents divorced, and I was introduced to various metaphysical types of spirituality by observing how my mother was experimenting in her own spirituality. Even though I have not been involved in religion since age twelve, I have since learned that you are imprinted with values and beliefs by the time you are eight years old; this programming will serve as the foundation of your life. (More reason for female hopelessness.) How do you change something that is imprinted? And how do you do that without role models and peers?

In most of my childhood years I felt alienated. Not only did I not belong to my familial religion and its members, but even my neighborhood and schools were predominantly made up of people from this religion, which strengthened my sense of alienation. I was also aware that I did not belong to anything else, and even if I did join another religious group, in my mind I would still be the outsider who converted. For some reason, the voice inside me kept pushing me to look for **my** tribe, the one I have always belonged to, and not the tribe that is chosen as a mere bandage for the pain.

As I matured, I found myself searching everywhere for clues, seeking tidbits that would "ring true." Although I never trusted another organized religion enough to join, I curiously researched many alternative spiritual practices, hoping to understand how other people find the "God connection." As a person with strong Virgo earth energy, I was instinctively led to the "**God connection**" in plants and their subtle, yet powerful, medicine. Not only does gardening heal and soothe the nerves, but plants offer so many pathways to healing a human body. I was naturally drawn to the understanding and acceptance of herbs, homeopathy, a healthy lifestyle, and healthy eating as something I didn't need to force. It just felt so right. Like a "God connection" would. This connection and wisdom felt true to me. The earth doesn't lie. Plants are innocent and yet hold so much wisdom. I innately knew this. This was a modality that, for me, had no **doubt** clouding it; rather purity enlightened it. The earth never marketed itself to me, it only gave to me freely. I trusted that.

Once I began a family, my maternal instincts spurred my learning in alternative healing modalities in order to keep my family healthy without relying on western (patriarchal) medicine. I also realized my leadership strengths were easily funneled into the confidence of using **alternative therapies**. I began my maternal years by trusting and learning about how women through the ages had taken care of their feminine needs by way of plants and intuition as well as tribal support. I had three amazing home births, and the last two were effortlessly unassisted, only because I was so in tune with my body and the wisdom it held beyond my mental understanding. Giving birth in this way was empowering. I was not only the leader of my experience, but I had the scholarly birth knowledge, the herbal/homeopathic support knowledge, and the trust in all the wise women and ancestors who had been doing this successfully for eons. I had identified the core feeling of trust in a power greater than my personal body and physical world. In essence the birthing process can be an experience with direct connection to God/Source.

I eventually became a doula (birthing assistant) for home birthing mothers. I studied and became skilled in specific support for pregnancy, labor, and lactation including herbal and alternative remedies or modalities to support the women and babies I served. I learned (or remembered) energy healing and the art of guided visualization to assist women in their process of building a strong body and trusting in the process of labor.

I felt more and more at home and complete, but not fully whole yet. As if all the nuggets I found only provided satisfaction temporarily. Being a doula is hard work and commitment, therefore after 10 years I decided to stop and focus on the gentle healing aspect of my learnings. I was now strengthening the trust and validation of my own intuition and the inner flow of God, Goddess, or Spirit that came through me for others gain. Because this flow already belonged to me, it came through me willingly. I gave myself permission to play and experiment, as if the so-called rules were just **guidelines anyway**. This allowed me to transform other models of energy work in order to fit my personal needs and likes. My inner child loved (and still loves) this freedom to play and be creative. I tapped into the essence of **Source Energy** that is **playful** and **free**. Just like nature, ever changing. I have enjoyed offering classes and guidance to others in using **Energetic Alchemy** or energy work as a way to change your current predicament or perceived issue, which is only an energy that is stuck and rigid. Most often it is not even yours. My drive is not to heal anyone, ever, but to guide people to their own healing abilities and offer them practices to change their own reality. I am a peer to them who reminds them that they have everything they need within. I am the person who remembers their strength, their connection to Source, and I simply show them the way. These techniques are but a few of many ways you may remember your strength, your connection, and your worthiness to receive in your life.

I have always been fascinated with Indigenous people and their practices; in truth, I was perhaps jealous of their spiritual "foundation." Even in the turmoil of horrendous genocide by foreign settlers, Indigenous people still maintained a heritage, a story that defines them and their purpose. This was something I had wanted in my life, and was perhaps something that I subconsciously missed. I found myself mesmerized, watching Indigenous practices from afar in **awe**. I sense a great **beauty** and **grace** in them as a human. I am forever grateful that more Indigenous peoples are now stepping into their roots and remembering their beautiful beginnings, teaching, practicing and honoring their sacred birth rights. Throughout my life, Indigenous cultures have been on the periphery for me: always nearby but out of my reach. I've known a few **Dine'** (Americans call Navajo) people in the past 20 years, but only briefly and superficially. I've been to a handful of pow wows and sacred Native areas, but still only as a curious spectator, an outsider. I have deep respect for their sacred ways, and I do not want to assume I have a right to pray or perform as they do. It is clear that my path is not to follow a Native American path. However, I do share in honoring the energies of the four cardinal directions and animal spirits.

In 2016, during a shamanic journey, I remembered several past lives as an Indigenous person from several different countries. I even became reacquainted with a graceful female Indigenous spirit guide who feels pre-Mayan or of that era. She has always been with me. Perhaps this is where my fascination lies.

It wasn't until 2014 that I was introduced to using a Medicine Wheel. A Medicine Wheel is a prayer space for Indigenous tribes that uses the four cardinal directions and the Sacred Circle as the basis. Medicine Wheels differ among the Native tribes, but they do have some similarities. I was lucky enough to enjoy and experience a beautiful Medicine Wheel that was on the property where I lived for eight years. I had the opportunity to learn about the creation, prayer practice, and use of this Sacred Circle. I began using this circle model in other areas of my spiritual life and became acquainted with the elemental directions, as well as the animal totem personalities. Creating relationships with the animal spirits (also involved in my shamanic journeying) has been another realm that offers the feel of support and tribe for me. For a year, as I traveled in a camper, I used the Sacred Circle and prayer with the four directions as a practice to shift or accelerate my personal transformations, as well as to perform ceremonies at the new and full moon cycles. I have especially enjoyed learning and playing with the Astrological eclipse energies within the Sacred Circle model. I have since been shown how many newly awakened souls are also bringing Archangels, Sacred Geometry and other high vibration energies into the Sacred Circle as well.

Using the Sacred Circle has been an easy and fun collaborative spiritual practice, because I collaborate with guides and spirit realm beings, that I have loved getting to know more intimately. It is so easy to set up, learn, and has unlimited potential. I felt inspired to share this technique with others in hopes for it to be a stepping stone to more, and to be a foundation to "bounce off of", as Esther Hicks would say.

"Once you know the basics of something;
you can build from there and expand
your spiritual creativity."

~ DEANNA KING

Changing nothing changes nothing.
Wishful thinking remains only a wish
without an equally powerful action.
Your action can then be amplified when
cooperatively used with the request and
invitation for Spirit to create with you.

~ DEANNA KING

Introduction

I'm writing this book for any individual who finds themselves suffering repercussions because of the people or situations that happen *around them or to them*. I am writing to YOU. You have probably noticed that layer of disempowerment that has crept into your life. It may be new, or it could have been with you since you can remember. You know, back in the beginning of your journey on planet Earth. Perhaps you feel as if you have little ability to fully change or accentuate the unfolding of your own life in the way you desire. Everywhere you turn now, there are self-help programs, self-help books, podcasts, and more. We are inundated with quick fixes, and a myriad of "life changing" and manifesting techniques. All of that self-help content, although heartfelt, insinuates that you're just not happy enough, not focused enough, or not something enough!

On the contrary, you are more than enough. And you have successfully been creating your life for a very long time; in fact you are a master creator. Perhaps you are already aware of how you have created in the past, or maybe you are unaware of the creating you've already done! No matter, NOW is the time to be a conscious and focused creator!

As someone who fell in love with the Law of Attraction ideas and techniques years ago, I completely understand that it is not usually second nature to make manifesting and positive feelings a part of your every waking moment. When I began using the Sacred Ceremony ritual with the Sacred Circle, I realized that the act of **creating the Ceremony** filled the need to have involvement of all my "bodies"... mind/body/spirit. In this practice, they are all involved at the same time. I was no longer using just my mind or my imagination. I was no longer just using my voice or my intent in prayer to invoke spirit. I was now incorporating my **activity** into the Ceremony and using my feminine creation energy to design the sacred space. My inner child was also let loose to play in the creation. **And** since I so often create the Circle in nature, I was also including the original Gaia Mother energy in the creation of the Ceremony. Suddenly, I felt the **wholeness** I had been looking for!

Many of us have had religious upbringings that no longer serve us or never served us, and perhaps some of us are still involved in religion on the periphery. You might be hanging onto it because you can't let it go just yet. If you are someone who relates to the loss of connection to "something you can't quite name," this book may help you to weave new fibers of connection.

A **Re-Membering** is in order.

Here are a few situations that may have affected your feeling of disconnection with spirit in your life today:

★ You feel like you no longer have a connection to spirit because you turned away from religion or religious people long ago due to trauma, rules/structure, dogma or any reason.

★ You recently (or for a long time) haven't liked the idea of religion and that has flavored your idea of spiritualism or 'God/Goddess/ Source.' You may feel that spirituality only involves religion.

★ You secretly know there is something greater than you, or within you, but it's not what you were taught, and it may not be called 'God.' Since you can't name it or define it, you don't know where to start with it.

★ You're not quite sure what you believe in, and therefore you don't give yourself credit to be curious and create what works for you.

★ You are interested in 'something bigger out there' but you don't know who to ask, or which group to connect with. Reaching out could be embarrassing, or intimidating and of course with our busy lives, who has time anyway?

★ You have memories or knowledge that you can't explain.

Whether your disconnection from your higher wisdom is due to your past experiences or is just an internal decision you have made as you've navigated life, this practice may help reclaim that connection to your higher wisdom. Even if you are someone who has a fulfilling spiritual life, using Ceremony may enhance and open new doors for you.

Ceremony and ritual are a part of human history; it lives in our ancestral line, it's in our DNA. No matter who you are on the planet, it already exists in you, dormant, like a seed waiting for spring. It is waiting for the right conditions to beckon it forth. When you let yourself play with the creation of Ceremony, your body and your soul begin to remember. You become **Re-Membered**. Something will take the lead. It's as if the ancestral part of you comes forward to be your elder in this timeframe, in this now.

I'm not offering you promises, I am offering you opportunities.

Ceremony and ritual are a means to a solution for challenges we face in life, such as when life says for example, "The job market is the dictator of your income and how far you can climb." You could just take that push back as truth and choose to be limited, or you could take **action**. Offering a Ceremony is one possible **action step** toward change. However, there are many other possibilities as well. No doubt in your life you have already tried a few and will continue to take on new practices as you age... trying new things is part of human maturing. This simple action step moves you towards **empowerment**. Towards a solution. Towards Re-membering.

Being human means, inevitably, that you are feeling limited in something. It's part of our wiring. It's as if we need a problem to solve or a wall to push against. Our ego needs problems in order to give it a purpose. Even if the purpose is simply to complain. We are creators and our ego is therefore equally creative. I'm sure you could name a few creative egos!

Egos like to be busy. Busy-ness can show up in many forms: it can be passive complaining while using social media or it can be knocking on doors for 8 hours until you make the sale. When we let the ego run itself, it often gets stuck in a non-solution rut. Especially now, with so much stress in our lives, we are all so exhausted just maintaining our lifestyles, so there is little vitality left for solution finding!

If you have fallen into the passive role of not taking productive action in some area of your life, take a break from any brooding over injustices for a moment and let your ego and your creative side have some fun for a change.

Grab a notebook and write out some of the answers to the questions that follow:.

★ Take a moment to ask yourself: where are you feeling limited right now?

Write it down and note how long this has been an irritation for you, whether it's a small voice in the background or a full blown "daily problem with the boss."

★ Where are you feeling a lack of wealth? (not necessarily money related)

Now consider these feelings. Imagine having a wealth of each of these words.

Ease	Flow
Abundance	Relief
Joy	Contentment
Confidence	Mastery
Choices	Opportunities
Miracles/Blessings	Reputation
Alignment	Rewards/Harvest
Accomplishment	Freedom
Permission	

Notice the feeling of the words.

Read them again, slowly this time. Feel each one. Notice it inside you.

They feel good. These words initiate a feeling that has no boundaries or limits.

Now, notice where you might want to expand your freedom in some of those areas.

★ Next write down: what is it you'd like to achieve or experience within each subject below, or write down if you are complete in that subject. This may give you some ideas for your upcoming Ceremony.

Relationships	Job/Career
Income	Housing
Passion/Gifts/Talents	Family/Children/Parents/Siblings
Community	Location
Health/Body/Mind	Connection with Spirit/Source/God/Goddess/Light/Love/Dimensions
Connection with Nature	

Now let's get clear on why you chose this book.

Learning how to use Sacred Ceremony offers a format for you to co-create with Spirit in order to create a new future, which then becomes the **new now**. I have used Ceremony to accentuate my own life decisions, the ones that I felt ill equipped for on my own. You know... when you get that weird feeling in your gut?

Somehow for me, Ceremony and the Spirit relationships I've forged have given me confidence. A confidence to know that I have a support system in the Spirit Realm. I AM NEVER ALONE. And I can always reach out, no matter what. In addition, the beautiful side benefit was that in the act of setting up the structure for the Ceremony, I became the designer of the "temple" for this **grand** event. It all then becomes a **vested** interest. It becomes an **act of Self Love**, where you will commune with Source and co-create **on your own behalf**.

'Isn't that selfish?' you might ask.

Well, when you are in an airplane and the oxygen masks are deployed, is it selfish to put an oxygen mask on yourself first before putting one on your child? No! It's merely the most practical choice. And you will be a far better you to share your love with others when you are feeling taken care of.

The act of being the 'creator' of the structure (whether it's in my yard or my living room) for such a beautiful event gave me purpose. I am a **creator**. And **so are you**!

Learning to use Sacred Ceremony offers you a framework to become reacquainted with the spiritual side of you while **also** enhancing your own life by using the forces of the Spiritual realm to assist with your dreams and/or assist the people you love. You don't need any classes or degrees, investments, weekend courses, or woo woo, just your curiosity. You got this!

Take a few moments to write out why you are attracted to Ceremony as a means to shift your life. List at least three reasons. For the overachievers out there, list as many as you want.

And most importantly, are you really ready to finish this book, to do a few ceremonies and give it an actual real investment of your time?

Yes, or no?

If you're not sure, then write what your hesitation might be. It might be your first Ceremony topic!

Great, I hope you now
have some more clarity!

MAGIC
Every day

Let the Magic begin!

(If you found yourself excited to start and skipped the introduction, please go back and do the exercise offered for clarity. It will be a game changer...)

I begin all important decisions with a prayer or invocation. Because heck, it actually MAKES a difference! I have experimented with this time and time again. It MAKES a difference. And with a verbal request for assistance, the situation I was focused on (or soon to be focused on) **always** went better, smoother, or even miraculously! By the way, I use the word "prayer" loosely, and differently than you probably were taught about prayer. If you are triggered by the word prayer, I get it, but please stick with me. Just breathe and open yourself up to a new idea of prayer. I used to get triggered by the word, but now the word has transformed into something magical for me.

LET THE MAGIC BEGIN!

This is my prayer for you and for this book:

"I call upon the blessings of The Supreme Being Source Light, and the All. I call for the blessings of Divine Mother Earth Gaia, the loving Mother. I call upon the Highest Deities that govern the Sacred Circle and the practice of Ceremony. May you bless this book endeavor with your light. May you touch the hearts of those ready for it. Let me be an open conduit for your wisdom and your laughter to flow through me. Let this transcript be full of hidden messages, deeper meanings, gratitude and creativity! May I speak and write the words that are most needed now for each person guided to this book. I thank you for your loving assistance. I thank you for sharing your Light. So be it. Thank you, thank you, thank you!"

Some part of you chose this book, so honor that. Close your eyes for a moment and ask yourself, "Where in my body does that part of me who chose this book reside?"

Notice the answer... just because.

I'm honored to be co-creating with you on this endeavor to your Re-membering of something more. Re-member the part of you who is aware. Re-member the part of you who knows about Ceremony, focus and choose a vibration that you need at this time in your journey.

I ask that you have an open heart and an open mind, let yourself expand into the realm of **curiosity**. I honor the curious and innocent nature within you that is always connected to the etheric world no matter what, even when you don't remember it.

Whether you know it or not, there is a part of you that knows more than you realize. In the next few pages, I will guide you through a process of building a physical structure that is a **foundation**. We build a foundation for your prayer, invocation (intention), and also a place for your connection to this so-called etheric realm. Together, we will reawaken your own personal knowledge of spirit. Please remember that this is a creative process, and just like an artist, we are playing with the colors and the medium. And, as all artists do, we are following our heart.

Most people, whether spiritual or not, remain stuck in the lot dealt to them, wishing for something different to show up. Waiting for someone else to take action. What if you needed to be the leader of your life? Believe it or not, taking a proactive and creative approach to amplify your intentions for change can be easy with a few simple guidelines and less time than we spend on an evening movie or social media.

~ DEANNA KING

CHAPTER 1

So... get to the point already! What is Ceremony?

IMPORTANT DEFINITIONS:

★ **Ceremony**: a formal act or series of acts prescribed by ritual, protocol, or convention.

★ **Invocation**: a prayer or request for the spiritual presence of Source/God/Goddess in a Ceremony or event. The summoning of a deity or the supernatural for assistance.

★ **Deity**: a god or goddess, one exalted or revered as supremely good or powerful.

I use the term Ceremony as a word to embrace a type of ritual that is using four components. These components will be described in the next four chapters.

Here is the basic breakdown of the four components:

★ The Sacred Circle.

★ The four directions.

★ The spirit realm.

★ Your personal invocation.

Although there are many types of beautiful ceremonies, some complex, we will be distilling the ritual down for ease and practicality. Because I told you I would make it easy, right? I promised this could be something you could do at home, with no investment or training. **Who needs to be trained for something their soul already knows anyway?**

My intent in writing this book is to bring the magic of ritual and Ceremony into the hands of **the people**. Real, everyday, amazing, people. People just like you, and your neighbor, and your friend. I hope that children will be included where possible, and therefore they will too become self-empowered. After all, they are the ones who we will all be depending on in the future. Let's empower them now in order to empower themselves. Sounds like a **win/win** to me.

I have to include a disclaimer...

I do not teach this from any religious perspective or even as a formatted Ceremony from any one culture. It is not my intention to be sacrilegious or disrespectful in any way of any Sacred Ceremony practice that exists on this planet. Every Sacred Ceremony has a place and a time. I honor that from my heart. I write purely from the directive of my higher wisdom. Bringing a complex procedure into the realm of ease for the masses. What is left is pure potential.

For those of you who are deeply touched and inspired from reading this book, it is my intention that you move forward and learn more about the more complex Ceremony rituals that are available to us from our Indigenous cultures and religious cultures. I trust **you** will know the truth of what you need.

Hallelujah for self-direction and instant gratification!

Performing the "Ceremony" can be as long or as short as you wish. As complex or as easy as you wish.

You get to drive this bus.

You get to orchestrate this production.

You get to choose the "color palette."

You may also choose to design it **alone** or in a **co-creative** way with others.

As I guide you, we will be using the Sacred Circle as the foundation in the Ceremony. There is a power in the circle. A circle to hold space, whether that space is **sacred** or **magic**. The circle becomes the boundary, or the **container** for this sacred experience.

CHAPTER 2

What is a Sacred Circle?

The Sacred Circle in ritual has been used for centuries, maybe longer, and is believed to have begun with the Matriarchal cultures. As magician and historian Jake Stratton-Kent writes, "In short, a circle is not an obsolete symbol of a superstitious fear of spirits, but an *intentionally created ritual space* for various purposes. It is not always required for all kinds of ritual work, but neither is it of no value, quite the contrary. Making sacred space is among the most primal of rituals, such intentional actions are as worthy of the term psychoactive as any substance."

Here are a few descriptions of a Sacred Circle:

★ "A Sacred Circle is a circle of space marked out by the practitioners of a ritual, in which they intend and believe will contain energy. The Circle forms a Sacred space, and will provide them a form of magical protection, or both."[1]

★ "The Sacred Circle is **a "traditional symbolic circle"** that incorporates the spiritual beliefs of many Indian tribes of North America."[2]

★ For many, the circle is **symbolic of equality, where no person is more prominent than any other person**."[3]

★ "The circle is the most common and universal sign, found in all cultures. It is the symbol of the sun in its limitless or boundless aspect. It has no beginning and no end, and no divisions, making it the perfect symbol of completeness, eternity, and the soul. The circle is also the symbol of boundary and enclosure, of completion, and returning cycles."[4]

★ "The Symbol meaning of a circle is universal, sacred and Divine. It represents the infinite nature of energy and the inclusivity of the universe."[5]

Not to be too big here, but yes, the inclusivity of the Universe.

Your circle. Not just any circle.

Who knew that something as seemingly simple could be so magnificent?

Here's more...

★ "The circle is a universal symbol with extensive meaning. It represents the notions of totality, wholeness, original perfection, the Self, the infinite, eternity, timelessness, all cyclic movement, God ('God is a circle whose center is everywhere and whose circumference is nowhere.)"[6]

Here is a quote from Black Elk on a wonderful post about circles by Margaret Bremner on her blog, Enthusiastic Artist:[7]

Black Elk, a medicine man and visionary of the Oglala Sioux, said,

"Everything the Power of the World does, is done in a circle. The sky is round and I have heard that the earth is round like a ball, and so are all the stars. The wind, in its greatest power, whirls. Birds make their nests in circles, for theirs is the same religion as ours. The sun comes forth and goes down again in a circle. The moon does the same, and both are round. Even the seasons form a great circle in their changing, and always come back again to where they were. The life of a man is a circle from childhood to childhood, and so it is in everything where power moves. Our tipis were round like the nests of birds, and these were always set in a circle; the nation's hoop, a nest of many nests where the Great Spirit meant for us to hatch our children."

So, there you have it. We will be starting with a circle. Simple. Beautiful.

You will now get to choose where your Ceremony will be. Will it be in your living room? Your backyard? You will want to make the first Ceremony circle large enough for you to easily walk around in. Consider six feet across or larger.

CHAPTER 3

Location, Location, Location

*N*ow let's begin with some action steps.

Location is somewhat important the first time. Choosing an environment that feels safe and loving is key. Consider the size you anticipate your Ceremony needs to be in order to pick the location – Ceremony is best to do in a large enough space for you or the people involved to walk around in or stand around the circle that is designated. I have used a medicine wheel circle as small as 3 feet across for myself only or up to 20 feet across for many people. Six to eight feet is a good medium.

Go ahead, pick a spot, or write down a few that would work for you. Is it private? Will there be interruptions? Is it free of clutter and inviting to you and spirit? And most importantly do you feel good in this place you have chosen?

CEREMONIES HELD INSIDE

If you have chosen for the first Ceremony to be in your house or a building, consider where you will set it up.

A spare bedroom or open space? A living room? A local church room? A space in your office or work? A friend's home space?

Begin the work...

a. Clean up the clutter in the room, and make the floor available for a circle of about six to eight feet.

This may involve moving furniture, vacuuming, and basic clean up.

How would you prepare if you were going to have the most important guests visiting?

b. Now create the ambiance with things like plants, lighting, candles, aromatherapy, crystals, tapestries, etc.

c. Cover the television or any other electronic items with a beautiful fabric, tapestry, or tablecloth. Yes, do it. Electronics have a certain energy which is not in alignment with our focus.

d. How does it feel to you when you are done? Are you happy with the *feel* of the space now?

CEREMONIES HELD OUTSIDE

If you have chosen for the first Ceremony to be outside, simply choose the location.

A backyard, a corner in the park, a community garden, out in nature, in places like the desert or the mountains, somewhere with a view, trees, or grass.

Now let's begin...

a. Choose a space that is inviting or will easily be inviting once you prep it. Hopefully a nice view is an option, since views are a plus but not necessary. Grass is super, since it's like a green, clean carpet. But if your spot has no grass, just make it feel beautiful. Maybe rake or smooth the dirt. If you are in your yard, spruce it up as if inviting important guests to visit. When you stand back and look at it, can you feel pride in where you have chosen? If you must move yard items out of the area, give five feet of distance between the circle edge and the items.

b. Creating the ambiance is next. Some ideas may be to place potted plants nearby, or to find a tree to perform the Ceremony under. If in your yard, look around to see where the best feeling area is, and how can you improve it with a little effort?

If you are outside in the "wild nature," just find a space that feels good. The tree spirits help a lot. You might need to clear away some branches or rocks to set the tone for the special space.

c. How does it feel to you when you are done? Are you happy with the *feel* of the space now?

Once you have decided where and have moved items out of the way or cleaned up the space, you are ready for the next step:

Energetic Cleansing of yourself, the environment and your sacred Ceremony space.

You and I possess within ourselves at every moment of our lives, under all circumstances, the power to transform the quality of our lives.

~ WERNER ERHARD

You are magical

CHAPTER 4

Cleansing your Sacred Space and Yourself

Cleansing or *purifying* is a practice of removing old stagnant or even negative energy and calling in fresh new energy. If you notice you feel *off* or drained after being around a lot of people, that's a good time to purify and reset with one or more of these items. I use them daily. There are several cleansing or clearing plants that will aid you. Choose the one or two that speak to you. Find them in a natural food store or online.

CALIFORNIA WHITE SAGE STICK/ DESERT MOUNTAIN SAGE STICK

The ritual of sage burning, also known as **smudging,** is an essential part of many Native American cultures. Burning sage is one of the oldest and purest methods of cleansing a person, group of people, or space and of getting rid of unwanted spirits. White Sage is known to clear bacteria in the air by way of its smoke. Sage smoke offers rapid delivery to the brain and efficient absorption into the body. Scientists have observed that sage can clear up to 94 percent of airborne bacteria in a space and disinfect the air. When sage is burned, it releases negative ions, which is linked to putting people into a positive mood. The Latin word for sage, *salvia*, stems from the word *heal*. Other qualities believed to be associated with sage when burned are giving wisdom, clarity, and increasing spiritual awareness.

HOW TO USE:

Open a window to let the smoke and any "bad juju" out. Using a lighter, start 1 leaf or 1 end of a sage stick **barely on fire;** it will continue to smolder, and you will put it out when you are done. Place the sage in a ceramic or stone bowl while it is smoldering (do not use plastic!) and move the sage and bowl around the room or the area you are working in with an intention to clear all the energy in the room all the way up into the corners. Also move the smoke around with your hand or a feather. Move it all around your whole body as well; don't forget your backside and your feet. If you feel body pains, clear or smudge those areas specifically. Use the smoke to also clear around your Ceremony circle and any items you may be using. Some people think Sage smells like marijuana, only weaker. Your clothes and home will smell of it. Just sayin'.

PALO SANTO WOOD

This sacred wood is from South America and may be endangered because of its popularity, so please purchase it wisely. A small stick will last a long time! This wood has a sweet smell. Again, this wood is lit, and the smoke is the clearing agent. Palo Santo does not stay lit as long as sage, so you may have to relight it during your clearing.

It is a powerhouse for clearing stagnant energy and creating a sacred space. This wood is used for both cleansing and restoring your energy. It is also known to attract abundance and good luck. Palo Santo is usually used during purifying rituals and during ceremonies to connect to spirit and surrounding positive vibrations. Not only does the smoke cleanse, but it also boosts morale. This multifaceted aspect is unique to Palo Santo — whereas some herbs like sage are used strictly for purification and wiping the slate clean, Palo Santo also infuses its *own* energy.

HOW TO USE:

Open a window to let the smoke and "bad juju" out. Using a lighter, start one end of the stick until smoldering. Palo Santo does not stay lit long and will need to be re-lit often during your cleansing. Place the stick in a ceramic or stone bowl or shell while it is smoldering (do not use plastic!) and move the Palo Santo and bowl around the room or the area you are working in with an intention to clear all the energy in the room all the way up into the corners. Move the smoke around the room with your hand, and move it around your whole body as well. Don't forget your backside and your feet! If you feel any body pains, make sure that the smoke reaches those areas specifically. Continue to clear around your Ceremony circle and any items you may be using.

If you want to go further, clear the whole house, each room, and around the outside of the house. For your yard, take the smoke to the edges of the yard and around the outside of your house/ building and property line.

ROSEWATER AND/OR FLORIDA WATER

These beautiful holy preparations have a high vibration and are sold in a misting spray bottle.

Rosewater is believed to have strong spiritual properties that can clear out negative energy that may be weighing you down. The scent of roses is often used in aromatherapy to give you a boost in positivity and a powerful mood enhancer. Rose petals carry a cooling nature, which can help support a balanced mind and heart. It relieves nervousness, grief, anger, low self-esteem and criticism. By eliminating feelings of anxiety and promoting emotional well-being, you become more relaxed. Roses have the highest vibration of all flowers and have been woven into sacred rituals and text for centuries due to their purity.

HOW TO USE:

Spray the air and furniture in all rooms with your intention to puri-fy. Outside, spray the area you will be working in, and don't forget to spritz yourself. Drink in the luxurious smell! Spray around your Ceremony circle and any items you may be using.

Florida Water is formulated with citrus essences, clove, lavender, and other herbal and floral extracts. It is aromatic and cleansing. Popular with the Southern Indigenous spiritual practices, it has also been used as a cologne!

HOW TO USE:

Florida Water does not come in a spray bottle, you can cleanse yourself by rubbing a drop or two of Agua de Florida in the palms of your hands and start by breathing it in. Then, pass your hands over your face and head, your chest, your back, and down your legs to your feet. In order to cleanse your house, you will need to transfer the liquid to a spray bottle. Then spritz the whole house and/or yard.

There you have it! Pick one or all and go about cleansing yourself and your Sacred Circle environment.

P.S. You **don't** have to have a Ceremony to use these cleansing tools, I use them as a morning ritual daily and throughout the day, depending on what is going on and who I have been around. It's a self-empowerment game changer!

If you happen to be in a pinch and can't purchase the items above or have to perform a Ceremony on the fly, use a candle and your intention to purify yourself as you move it over your body and around the space. I've also just invoked assistance from the higher realms to cleanse in a pinch, like when you are in the woods and have no sacred items with you because you didn't know you might want to do a Ceremony. I've also pulled over to the side of the road and performed a Ceremony because I was inspired to. The more you do this, the more you become attuned to the vibration of clearing. When you are attuned, you can invoke the shift just by being familiar with the energy of the clearing agents and the Ceremony Practice, although I prefer to use the items listed whenever I am near to them. The smell of the sacred clearing items are in and among themselves very therapeutic, healing, and transforming.

"Shields Up"
Creating an Energetic Shield

You will want to create an energetic shield in **addition** to the previous clearing practices. I create a shield every morning or again when I'm in the presence of intense energy, and sometimes that is just at the grocery store!

Sit quietly and focus on your heart and the connection you have with Divine Mother Earth. Visualize your body being surrounded by a white luminous light. Say to yourself, "I now create and activate my shield of light to be impenetrable to all negative energies. My shield of light allows positive energy to flow out and to flow in." See and feel the light around you, and now that it has been created, just announce, "Shields up!" and viola, protection activated.

Next, we will spend some time crafting your prayer or intentions that will be spoken to the spirit realm during the Ceremony. This will become part of your invocation. This preparation will get you focused on what it is you desire to change.

Once you make a decision,
the universe conspires to make it happen.

~ RALPH WALDO ANDERSON

Moonchild

CHAPTER 5

Crafting your Prayer/Invocation

THE "GETTING CLEAR" PHASE

First, we must get clear on why you want to perform a Ceremony for yourself or someone else.

The first time you do something new like this always takes more time. Keep in mind that, as you get the hang of it, you won't need to prepare your words as much; you will simply be able to state it from your heart in the moment. So give yourself permission to take the time needed to craft your intentions for the first few times.

Find an opportunity where you will have at least an hour. You will also need a notebook. Answer the following questions in order to get clearer about why you are going to perform a Ceremony. Again, this is probably only for the first few times until you feel confident in the whole process. Please consider all of the following questions.

Why do you want to do this particular Ceremony today? Break it down into one sentence.

★ Ex. I desire to ease my child's trouble with school.

★ Ex. I want to make more money, either in the same job or a different job/side job of $_____.

★ Ex. I want to assist in sending healing for _____.

★ Ex. I wish to let go of _____.

★ Ex. I want help making a decision regarding _____.

★ Ex. I want to attract and/or move on from a relationship.

★ Ex. I want to buy/sell/move house.

★ Ex. I am celebrating... menarche, rites of passage, marriage, graduation, moving, or business.

★ Ex. I am letting go of someone who has now passed; I lovingly let go of them.

★ Ex. I want assistance with a law, tax, or debt problem of _____.

★ Ex. I wish to expand my psychic or creative abilities.

★ Ex. I wish to heal from and let go of childhood trauma of _____ (get as specific as possible here).

★ Ex. I want to forgive someone and find peace within myself.

★ Ex. I wish to feel more powerful, confident, and love myself.

★ Ex. I wish to receive the loan on my terms (get as specific as possible here).

★ Ex. I wish to transform my hobby or passion into my profession.

Answering this next question will help you get clear on your intent.

★ Will this request hurt anyone else or negatively impact them?

Be honest! If so, you need to revise your intention so you will not willfully be hurting anyone. For example: "I want my coworker to get fired so I can move up." A healthy revision would be "I want to move into a place of more authority and prestige within my career. I am open to the best solution for everyone involved, even if I have to change jobs." Often, when you make a request from a place of integrity, Spirit may just in fact offer the other person a new job... and viola, your position is free to move into! It can be that easy.

Keep this in mind. When you make a request and it **will** ultimately be hurting others, Spirit or your higher self does not want to be entangled with energy of malintent and selfishness. Own your Integrity! Be fair and just to both yourself and others. This is, after all, an act of trust that there is enough for everyone. Period.

★ How will this improve your life or another person's life (specifically, the person you are performing the Ceremony for)?

Get real here... a surface answer would be something like: "I'll have more money." A deeper answer would be, "I'll be using my strengths to grow and help others; the money will be rewarding me for my efforts to improve myself and this job. I can push myself to become more than who I am now."

★ List five reasons why you want to improve your (or someone else's) life with this intention?

You get the gist here, go deep with your answers.

★ Will this wish or intention enhance your ability to make others' lives better?

★ What have you already done in an attempt to create this?

Here are some examples:

I've been talking to my boss; I've been looking in the 'Help Wanted' ads; I've improved my resume; I've taken classes; I've talked to influential people; I've listened to positive affirmations; I've done counseling to uncover my wounds; I've stopped bad habits in order to be grounded; I've quit spending money on stuff that I don't really need; I've begun an exercise program; I've meditated on it for four weeks; I've made more room in my life by quitting "xyz"; I've had a healing session focused on it; I've done a bunch of research and gotten clear on what I really want and need; I've gotten real with myself about any denial; I've lovingly told the truth about how I felt to the other people involved.

Just in case you aren't sure, "I've wanted it for a really long time..." is **not** an attempt at creating what you want. We are looking for action steps.

★ How will your life be different if you achieve this?

Answering this will help you craft what you want to change in yourself.

★ What has been holding you back from receiving or creating this already?

Discuss this in a way that does not involve blaming others. This would be most effective as "I" statements. Taking responsibility for where **you** are, not anyone else.

More examples:

I see that I am afraid; I have a poverty or victim consciousness; I don't trust life to bless me; My upbringing didn't support me to function like this; I made a mistake and I don't know how to change it; I can't forgive someone; I'm angry; I don't trust that life can be good; I let them manipulate me; I said yes because I wanted to be liked but now it's no longer good for me; I need to make more money for this to happen; I'm living beyond my means; I'm confused about how to change; I need a helper or guide; I don't feel this community supports me; I'm lost in the competition; I'm intimidated by the housing market; I'm afraid of failure; I don't know how to change it.

So hopefully, after answering those questions, you're clearer about yourself and your intentions. Clarity is always good.

Now we move into creating your Prayer and Invocation. These words are sometimes used interchangeably, but here is a small idea of the meanings of Prayer and Invocation.

PRAYER[8]

★ a devout petition to God or an object of worship (like a statue).

★ a spiritual communion with God/Spirit.

★ the act or practice of praying to God/Spirit.

INVOCATION[9]

★ the act of invoking or calling upon a deity, spirit, etc., for aid, protection, inspiration, or the like; supplication.

★ any petitioning or supplication for help or aid.

★ a form of prayer invoking God/ Spirit's presence, especially one said at the beginning of a religious service or public Ceremony.

★ an entreaty for aid and guidance from a deity, etc.

★ the act of calling upon a spirit.

★ the magic formula used to conjure up a spirit; incantation.

THERE ARE SEVERAL PARTS TO THE INVOCATION OR PRAYER:

★ Call in the four directions to assist in holding space (explained later).

★ Call in the spirits to help you.

★ State your request. Why are you doing this Ceremony? **See your answer from question number 1 in the Getting Clear Phase of Chapter 5.**

★ Offer your gratitude.

★ Release the resistance energy.

EXAMPLE #1: INVOCATION

Here is an example from the first question from the "Getting Clear" phase.

Question: "Why do you want to do this particular Ceremony today?"

Example Answer: "I want to easily find and buy land for less than $40,000 that has a stunning view, large trees, and the zoning I require."

This is the Invocation I crafted from the above statement. It includes the calling in of spirit, the explanation of my request, and the letting go of why I haven't achieved it yet and my resistance to receiving it. It ends with gratitude. The underlined words are how we addressed the specifics for our request in this Ceremony.

Call in the spirits:

"I call upon the blessings of The Supreme Being, Light and Love. I call upon the Blessings of Mother Earth Gaia, the beautiful force that I come from. May you hear me, be with me and assist me on this endeavor today. I call in my own higher guides that are assisting me to grow to my full potential."

State your request:

"I Invoke your love and assistance, with the ease in finding the right property for me with beautiful mature trees, a view I love, the appropriate zoning, and at $40,000 or less. Keep me comfortable until I am living there, let me trust you are supporting me all the way. (Part of question #8). Let this be for the highest good for everyone involved."

Offer Gratitude and release what is not serving you:

"I receive your guidance, your wisdom, your love and your highest good for me. I am grateful for the shifting and letting go of the **fear** of not securing a nice piece of land for this price. I lovingly let go of any **beliefs** I have about unworthiness and missing out on the right timing. I **trust** that you are providing for me, and that I am worthy. (From question #8 on the "Getting Clear Phase"). Help me to hear your guidance and act on it.

I am grateful for the ease in transforming my worthiness limits and receiving the land I love. (From question #7). Thank you, Thank You, Thank you."

Note that, I underlined both the statements that are directly speaking to the desired shift and the statements that may be holding me back from receiving it. These are #1 and #8 from "Getting

Clear Phase". See your own notes for how you answered all the questions.

Next, be sure that you are able to state in a positive way *what you need to transform*. This has to do with how you answered question #7.

Notice how I stated "letting go of fear of not getting a nice piece of land for this price. I lovingly let go of any beliefs I have about unworthiness and missing out on the right timing. I trust that you are providing for me, and that I am worthy."

In this statement, I take full responsibility for the fact that I have fear, that I have an unworthiness belief that is causing me to feel fear about getting something good for a lower price, and that I don't trust I can find it in the time I need.

It is important to acknowledge your own shortcomings, especially those that are creating your current situation. Self-responsibility is a *Super Power* that will transform almost any victim energy you have. You are using this opportunity to change where you know you need to shift.

Here is the full Invocation.

"I call upon the blessings of The Supreme Being, Light and Love. I call upon the Blessings of Mother Earth Gaia, the beautiful force that I come from. May you hear me, be with me and assist me on this endeavor today. I call in my own higher guides that are assisting me to grow to my full potential.

I Invoke your love and assistance, with the ease in finding the right property for me with beautiful mature trees, a view I love, the appropriate zoning, and at $40,000 or less. Keep me comfortable until I am living there, let me trust you are supporting me all the way. Let this be for the highest good for everyone involved.

I receive your guidance, your wisdom, your love and your highest good for me. I am grateful for the shifting and letting go of the **fear** of not getting a nice piece of land for this price. I lovingly let go of any **beliefs** I have about unworthiness and missing out on the right timing. I **trust** that you are providing for me, and that I am worthy. Help me to hear your guidance and act on it.

I am grateful for the ease in transforming my worthiness limits and receiving the land I love. Thank you, Thank You, Thank you."

Example #2: Invocation

Here is another example of an answer to question #1 from the getting clear phase.

"I wish to easily receive the money owed to me by Joe, in an efficient manner for everyone involved. I wish to receive the full amount and more. I wish to be surprised with how it all transpires."

To Repeat: This is the Invocation I crafted from the above statement. It includes:

★ The calling in of spirit and helpers.

★ The explanation of my request.

★ The letting go of why I haven't achieved it yet or my resistance to receiving it.

★ Allowing love and guidance now.

★ It ends with gratitude.

"I call upon the blessings of The Supreme Being, Light and Love. I call upon the Blessings of Mother Earth Gaia, the beautiful force that I come from. May you hear me, be with me and assist me on this endeavor today. I call in my own higher guides that are assisting me to grow to my full potential.

I Invoke your love and assistance, with the transfer of money owed to me. Assist this transaction to be in ease and understanding. Let this be in the highest good for everyone involved. I ask to receive the full amount and more in a way that blesses me in all ways, and I wish to be surprised with the results.

I receive your guidance, your wisdom, your love and your highest good for me. I am grateful for the shifting and letting go of fear. I lovingly let go of any beliefs about scarcity or punishment. (From question #8).

I am grateful for the ease in ending an old agreement and being blessed with financial support. (From question #7). Thank you, Thank You, Thank you."

Notice how I stated, "Letting go of fear. I lovingly let go of any beliefs about scarcity or punishment." Again, I take full responsibility for the fact that I do have fear, that I have a scarcity belief that is what is causing me to feel scarcity!

Watch out for childish or immature statements that are selfish or blame others. There is no room in Ceremony for selfishness or blame.

For example:

I did not say, "Make them be more generous, help them to see my way."

I did not say, "I am grateful for finally getting the money they owe me," "I am grateful to be done with this unfairness."

You are an adult, so we will choose to act with integrity. Spirit is connected to the higher path with an open heart and truth. That is where you will be during the Ceremony and hopefully afterwards too!

Next I have a blank invocation for you to fill in...

BLANK INVOCATION:

"*I call upon the blessings of The Supreme Being, Light and Love. I call upon the Blessings of Mother Earth Gaia, the beautiful force that I come from. May you hear me, be with me and assist me on this endeavor today.*

I Invoke your love and assistance, with _____

_____

_____

_____

Assist this request to be in _____

(ease and understanding?). Let this be in the highest good for everyone involved.

I ask to receive _____

_____

_____

_____

I receive your guidance, your wisdom, your love and your highest good for me. I am grateful for the shifting and letting go of

_____

_____

_____

I am grateful for the ease in ending

_____

_____

_____

Thank you, Thank You, Thank you."

Changing it up

What if you want to call in certain Deities you work with or are needing for this situation?

Maybe you already identify with Kali, the female goddess who is known as a badass and who can get a bit angry (for good reason of course). Or maybe you want to call in Ganesha, the Hindu god who can remove obstacles? Perhaps you have an affinity with snake energy and wish to shed your old skin, or if you want to commune with Archangel Michael who is a master at cutting energetic cords. **Yes, Yes, Yes** they all want to be invited in your special endeavor! So, if this speaks to you, craft them into your invocation.

This calling in of additional Deities would be added after you call in Mother Earth but before you invoke their love and assistance for your intention.

Examples of other Deities and guides you may wish to call on include:

FEMININE ENERGIES

★ **Kali:** Invokes healthy anger and standing up for yourself.

★ **Quan Yin:** Goddess of compassion.

★ **Mother Mary:** Nurturing feminine mother energy.

★ **Lakshmi:** Goddess of abundance.

Example: I call in the Divine Feminine Energies of Kali, Quan Yin, and Mother Mary. Bless me with your nurturing Feminine wisdom. Let me receive more nurturing and know when to give.

MASCULINE ENERGIES

Archangel Michael: Protector, can rid you of parasite energy or cords.

Buddha: Great compassion and surrendering.

Archangel Metatron: Builder of Sacred Geometries, angel of immense power and wisdom.

Jesus Christ or Christ force: Divine Light and Love.

Example:

I call in the Divine Masculine Energies of Archangel Michael, Buddha, Metatron, and Jesus Christ to assist me with protection and action. Let me know the security you provide and allow me to be courageous and act on my desires. Clear me of harmful energies or beliefs.

YOUR OWN PERSONAL GUIDES OR ANCESTORS

You may call in Grandparents or other ancestors by name.

You may call in the name of your spirit guide if you know it or just ask for "my Spirit Guides."

Example: I call in _____ to bring to me your support and wisdom.

Now let's get ready to define the Sacred Circle.

Being the Authority of your life is easier with instructions and a Model as a starting point. Using Ceremony as your model to implement change for yourself or others is a great beginning in taking charge of your own life and how it plays out. YOU become the Ceremony director. Ceremony is the structure that brings action into your wishes. Spirit powers it up for that extra punch. And now you have a tangible and creative process that creates change. Ceremony offers a "place to connect with spirit", that is free from religion or dogma. Ceremony can be individualized and unique to your needs and desires.

~ DEANNA KING

CHAPTER 6

Defining the Sacred Circle

Decide how you are going to define your Sacred space and be ready to embody your highest Creative Self. **Let your Super Powers Flow!**

Defining the circle can be as simple as four rocks to mark four equal points or it can be more complex, such as using many items to create an imaginary circle line. If you are doing this outside, you could go so far as using spray paint to draw the circle onto the grass or ground. Others have even used a rope or tape as the circle marker. So let your inner creator out!

Here are some questions for your **Creator Self**:

★ Do you want to create your Sacred Circle on either the floor, grass, dirt, or gravel etc.?

★ Do you want to use a nice fabric to place your circle onto? Of course, if you have a pretty rug, that works great. However, I have also used sarongs, tablecloths, blankets, sheets, or just nice fabric pieces. Fabric does not always lay flat, so you decide what feels best. Remember that you are the artist.

What will be in your circle?

Try this to start.

THE TREASURE HUNT

Go on a treasure hunt in your house and yard. Gather a few favorite items that you love, or are special, or maybe things that give you a warm feeling.

This may include flowers, herbs (fresh or dried), crystals, pretty rocks, feathers, twigs, shells, leaves, a candle, a written quote (printed or one you write down), a small photo, animal statues, pine branches, or other special items. Putting small mementos from loved ones will imbue their energy and blessings into the circle as well. **Have fun!** Also consider what each item means to you and how it will enhance the circle and your endeavor. I even put money in the circle sometimes, or powerful words. I've made the border of the circles using wood twigs, or the combination of many items. Below you will see a list of items that represent the four cardinal directions; you may keep that in mind as well.

Some other examples of things that you could put in your Sacred Circle are:

★ A picture of your dream home.

★ A paper with "Congratulations on your new job."

★ A wedding photo if you want to manifest a successful relationship.

★ A thinner picture of you if you are losing weight.

★ A photo of that big vacation.

★ A bestseller's photo if you are a writer.

Choose which items will mark the four cardinal directions; the rest are filler and go in between the four major directions. (See below for more details on the directions and their associations.)

Once you have your items, you may begin to place them in your circle. Figure out the directions of north, south, east, and west. You may use an app on your phone, or if you have a great sense of direction you can just go with your own inner knowing. We all know the sun rises in the east, after all! I always start with the east because it is the beginning of the day and in the circle it represents the beginning of cycles.

Start with the four directions and begin in the east. Next, mark the south, west, and north points of your circle. Be sure they are defined and at least 6 foot across. For example, east should be 6' from west and north should be 6 feet from south.

The Four Directions

East represents air, the new day, spring, and wisdom. What reminds you of east? A feather or an eagle photo? Or just a powerful-feeling stone that reminds you of the new dawn? Place your item here.

South represents fire, the summer, the sun, willpower, and action. Do you feel compelled to place a candle here, or a yellow or orange stone or flower? How about a powerful word like "action," or summer fruits? Place your item here.

West represents water, the fall, emotions, and the moon. Perhaps you would place a shell, or a bowl of water, something blue, or an ocean totem at the western point of your circle. Place your item here.

North represents earth, winter, the body, completion or resting, and fertility. I like to use dark stones to remind me of the north's earth energy. But a bowl of soil or a horn, winter foods, a photo of the earth, or a small plant are all great options as well. Place your item here.

Then fill in the spaces in between the four cardinal directions with your other items. You also may want to make an inner circle closer to the center and an outer circle.

CREATIVE IDEAS

Sometimes I put a small Buddha in the center, or even a quartz crystal to power the energy. I also like quartz crystals as markers for the places in between the directions because crystals hold a high vibration. Just remember that there is no absolute right way to create your Sacred Circle. You get to decide what feels right for you. Your Ceremony style will change and be slightly different each time, so give yourself freedom to go with the flow and with what wants to happen today.

Once you have finished "creating" your Sacred Circle, step back and *feel* it.

How does it feel? Make any changes necessary to help it feel really good to you.

Offer gratitude for each beautiful item you placed there and how they are assisting you. Give yourself gratitude for taking these steps.

(If you have invited guests to be a part of your Ceremony, you would most likely be waiting for them to arrive now, unless you invited them to create the circle with you.)

Most important is to cleanse **Each Person's Energy** with the sage or other item as they enter the home or yard. If they have brought an item for the Ceremony, let them place it, and ask them to take their places around the circle.

Now we prepare to invite Spirit and the four directions into the circle...

You can get to where you want to be from wherever you are - but you must stop spending so much time noticing and talking about what you do not like about where you are.

~ ESTHER HICKS

The Essential Law of Attraction Collection

Be magic

CHAPTER 7

Invocation of Spirit and the Cardinal Four Directions

BLESSING THE CIRCLE

Please read this whole chapter before you begin so that you know what to expect or how to make any changes. Prior to this step you would have cleansed the room or outdoor space and have announced, "Shields Up."

Have your invocation paper with you, the one you crafted previously.

The following is the outlined steps when you are beginning the Ceremony, after you have created the Sacred Circle. You will refer back to this chapter for each Ceremony, to Invoke the Spirit Helpers and move around the Sacred Circle.

STANDING OUTSIDE THE CIRCLE:

★ Grab your clearing agent (sage, Palo Santo, etc.) and light it once more.

★ Cleanse yourself again, as well as your invocations papers.

★ Cleanse the circle space by walking around the outside of it.

Now, step inside the circle from the **east**.

★ Stand facing east while holding your cleansing agent. Travel clockwise. (So if east is considered 12 noon, walk toward 3pm, which is south, then 6pm, which is west, and then 9pm, which is north.)

★ Walk around the inside parameter one time while using your chosen cleansing agent to cleanse the interior of the circle.

★ Use your intention to *really own* this space as sacred for yourself as you walk around to each of the directions. Think or state out loud, "I clear any and all energies that are not in alignment with my intentions."

Then when you get back to the east, stop. Facing east, you may begin the invocation of the four directions, starting with east. Again, you will be traveling clockwise during this stage.

Facing east, put your arms up to the sky.

"I call in the Energy of the East,

I call in the dawn and new beginnings, I call for the Element of Air, Breath, Wind, and Thought.

I call in the winged ones, and the higher perspective they have. I ask for your wisdom and perspective today. I call in the Energy of Spring and the power of life force germinating in the spring.

I am blessed by your presence."

Walk to the south, facing south, put your arms up to the sky.

"I call in the Energy of the South,

I call in the Summer, the Element of Fire, Willpower, and Action.

I call in the Coyote energy to remind me to not take life too seriously.

I ask for your support and blessings to fuel my actions and to easily find my true voice to speak up.

I am blessed by your presence."

Walk to the west, facing west, put your arms up to the sky.

"I call in the Energy of the West,

I call in the Autumn, the harvest, The Element of Water, Emotions, and the Feminine Moon.

I call in the water beings, and the Bear energy. Thank you for the wisdom you bring to the earth. I ask for your support to be flexible, nurturing, strong, and in touch with my emotional self.

I am blessed by your presence."

Walk to the north, facing north, put your arms up to the sky.

"I call in the Energy of the North,

I call in the Winter, a time to go within. I call in the Element of Earth, The physical plane.

I call in the Nature beings and Buffalo. Let me receive your sustenance.

I ask that you support my body to be grounded and resilient. Bring me your strengths.

I am blessed by your presence."

Now go to the center of the circle.

Standing close to the center, you will be stating the purpose of your Sacred Ceremony today, as you have written it earlier. Use your intuition as to what direction you want to face, perhaps even directing your invocation inward to your own heart.

Begin your Invocation

"I ask for the blessings of The Supreme Being, Light and Love. I call upon the Blessings of Mother Earth Gaia, the beautiful force that I come from...

(Optional: now you may invoke any other elements, spirits, or deities you wish to be present and assist this endeavor.)

Now state the remainder of the invocation you crafted. This is the reason for the Ceremony.

Finish

"Thank you for hearing me today and helping our hearts to connect and be one."

Stand for a moment and let yourself feel gratitude.

Close the circle when you're done. The closing of the circle is how we pay respect to all deities you have invited, one at a time, like this:

"Thank you (Deity's name) for your assistance, I release you now."

Thank the elements, starting in the east and going clockwise to the north.

Stepping to the east, facing east

Thank you, all energies in the East.

I gratefully let you all go; I gratefully release this energy to you.

Stepping to the south, facing south

Thank you, all energies in the South.

I gratefully let you all go; I gratefully release this energy to you.

Stepping to the west, facing west

Thank you, all energies in the West.

I gratefully let you all go; I gratefully release this energy to you.

Facing north

Thank you, all energies in the North.

I gratefully let you all go; I gratefully release this energy to you.

So be it. Thank you, Thank you, Thank you!

Here are some alternative endings that you may use at the end of your invocation.

★ Aho.

★ Namaste.

★ It is done.

★ Amen.

★ So it is.

You may now either step out of the circle in the east direction or take a moment to witness this beautiful event. You may sit in the circle and *relish* in what has just transpired, *feeling* all the energy in there.

When you are ready, you may step out through the east and begin to put things away. There is no hurry, but do not let others walk on it before you put it away.

If you had others attending the Ceremony, everyone would step out and hold hands to feel the blessings for 1–3 minutes. Then thank each other. Breathe and begin a celebration within your hearts. You may either go to another area to discuss or quietly begin to dismantle the circle.

True prayer is neither a mere mental
exercise nor a vocal performance.
It is far deeper than that -
it is a spiritual transaction with the
Creator of Heaven and Earth.

~ CHARLES SPURGEON

CHAPTER 8

The Checklist

Here is a brief outline and checklist to assist you during your first few Ceremonies.

THE OFFICIAL FORMAT OF HOW IT ALL COMES TOGETHER

★ Make a copy of and fill in the following list.

★ Read the whole page before beginning.

CHECKLIST

Location is _____

Examples include the living room, my house, friend's house, backyard or outdoor area, mountains, lake, or park.

Date is _____

Time is _____

List of people to invite (if pertinent) _____

_____

_____

_____

_____

Contacted them with RSVP?

Yes   No

How many are coming? _____

Size of the circle identified (circle one):   3 ft. 6 ft. 9ft. 12ft.

Larger (write size here) _____

Invocation is written and ready?

Yes   No

Do I have all items needed (clearing agent/items for circle)?

Yes   No

Preparing the preceding checklist can be done at any time prior to the Ceremony, even days before, as long as you have all of the information needed. But once you begin to *create the circle* as discussed below, you will need to be starting (and finishing) the whole Ceremony at that time because you are clearing/cleansing and building the circle. You want to keep the momentum going with the full invocation and closing shortly after you have made the circle.

For example, do not build your circle on a Saturday but wait for a later day to call in the spirits. That would create a break in the flow. So, be prepared to perform your Ceremony once you create the circle. Once you start the preparation of the Sacred Circle below, immediately move into the performing of the Ceremony.

PREPARING THE SACRED CIRCLE

I cleansed and ground myself with the clearing agent(s)?

Yes   No

I cleansed the perimeter of the home or yard?

Yes   No

I cleansed the area of the circle?

Yes   No

I created the Sacred Circle?

Yes   No

PERFORMING THE CEREMONY

(You don't have to check these off as you go; just be aware of what you will need to be doing and the order of the steps.)

Did I open the space and connect to spirit, starting with the four directions?

Yes   No

Did I state the invocation?

Yes   No

Did I close the Ceremony by thanking the Spirits and directions?

Yes   No

Now it's time to step out of the circle and *feel gratitude in your heart!*

Congratulations, you're done! It's time to celebrate!

Always Re-member, You got this!

"Where two or more of you are gathered there I am."

~ MATTHEW 18:20

CHAPTER 9

Inviting others – Group Ceremony

By the time you are reading this chapter, you have a feel for what is involved and how it may all play out. Maybe you've even done a Ceremony by yourself. Now is the time to decide if you are ready for the added blessing of inviting other individuals into your sacred Ceremony space.

Why would I invite others?

1. Because they will enhance the manifestation for everyone.

2. Because they wholeheartedly support the person the Ceremony is for.

3. Because there is a mutual benefit for them to come, it's a win/win all around.

Answer these questions as you consider who you want to invite.

★ Who will be invited? Practice utmost discernment. It does not serve you or your intention to invite naysayers or those looking for entertainment. This is not a multilevel marketing party. More is not better. Make a list of people who you are interested in inviting and narrow it down to the most beneficial six or eight.

It's important to be clear about why the individuals you pick are a benefit to the overall energy of the Ceremony.

★ Can they...
Support your own intentions? More people means more energy.

For example, you want to start a career in art, and your friends love your art and want to support you making this change. Invite those people!

★ Can they...
Support someone else for whom the Ceremony is for?

For example, my daughter is becoming a woman and I want her close friends and meaningful adults to honor, witness, and celebrate her passage.

★ Can they...
Support the group intent whole-heartedly?

For example, it's a new moon Ceremony and these individuals want to do it with you in order to bless themselves, another, each other, and the collective with their wishes.

Now that you have a list of people, you need to be clear about why you are inviting them. Next to each person's name, fill in the answers to these questions.

★ Why did you choose them and why or how do you feel they will enhance this Ceremony?

★ Is this person able to hold sacred space? (Yes, no, or maybe?)

★ Will they add to the beauty and purpose of this Ceremony? Or are they just a warm body?

You will find some people are super stoked to come to your Ceremony and will make all kinds of promises. But seriously, if you don't have personal experience with them, this is not the situation to get to know them unless someone else can vouch for them or you just get that good feeling about them. Use your discretion and discernment wisely. There will always be more ceremonies and if they are really interested they will stick around.

Exercise your discernment. Don't invite naysayers or even enthusiastic placeholders! Your Ceremony is not for anyone's entertainment. This is not the event that someone chooses because they are bored and need something cool to do. Invite those people that are already respectful.

Can you answer the following question with a resounding, "Yes!"?

★ Does this person have a good celebratory intention, or a heart connection to supporting the person or topic that the Ceremony is for? Are they honored to offer their good juju and love?

Again, I must say" "Use discernment wisely!"

Negative energy is **negative** energy.

★ **Definition of a Naysayer:** one who denies, refuses, opposes, objects, gossips about or criticizes something.[10]

They are not someone you'd want at your Ceremony, right?

We all know those people. I hope you are letting those people drop away from your life so that you may shine as more of your cheerful, authentic self. Please don't consider inviting them, even if they plead and say they will behave.

Hmmm, maybe that is a topic for a Ceremony?

Lastly, I have to add...

★ Can they be sober?

Oh, yeah I did write that. It's a touchy topic so here is my understanding. Mood altering is *consciousness altering*. Drugs and alcohol have a place, but not in Ceremony. This is not a party, not a show, not a "let's get high and see spirits" gig, and it's not a Sacred Ayahuasca Ceremony either. (That is a whole other realm.) So make a commitment to do that stuff at another time in another venue, and ask your supporters to do the same. Being in your body is part of showing up in *integrity*. We're talking about one to two hours here. So just be you, beautifully unaltered.

What about the person who is curious? This is your decision to make. If you take them through the above criteria and they pass, great! It's always good to open new avenues for people! But don't get involved in becoming their *weekend entertainment*.

Once you have your list, keep in mind that you can't *control* what others do or how they act. It's simple. If they do something uncomfortable, just don't invite them again.

Three examples would be...

1. They told you they would come sober and you sensed they were high or they admitted that they "only smoked a little."

2. They made a comment, sigh, or eye roll during the process that felt disrespectful or that was made in a judging manner.

3. They interrupted your process or disregarded something and it just didn't seem like an innocent mistake.

Keep in mind that anyone who is not **giving to** the Ceremony, *is* instead **taking energy from** the Ceremony. This is not helpful. That would be filed in the category of negative energy.

Great! Now you can make your list and invite these lucky and special souls!

The first time around, consider starting with just four or fewer people.

Can they be part of the set up?

Yes! Let them help you set up the circle so they feel included and have a creative invested interest in the sacred space. It's also nice to have people take on tasks like clearing the room with your clearing agent or clearing the other guests with the sage or Palo Santo. Or better yet, maybe you want to have a potluck meal afterward and they could all help clean up.

Where do all these people stand during the Ceremony?

When you do Ceremony with a group, it's nice to have them stand on the outside of the outer circle with you on the inside calling in the four cardinal directions and stating the invocations. They could also be on the inside, but only if your circle is really large, around 20 feet. In that case, they would be on the inside but at the outer edge, leaving room for you to walk around the interior.

WAYS YOU MAY INCLUDE THE GROUP IN THE CEREMONY

When you are performing a Ceremony for others like a rite of passage or request for health, here is an idea regarding how to include them.

The people invited could bring a story or item that is related to the individual and share it or place it in the circle.

For any personal Ceremony, you can include a group in other ways.

★ They could bring items for the circle, such as glitter, crystals, ribbons, a tapestry, candles, or even food for before or after the Ceremony.

★ They could bring a pertinent poem or gratitude letters to you and your gifts.

★ They could bring fabrics to drape in the room or on yourselves.

★ They could bring items of adornment, animal statues, wisdom about animal totems to invoke, or plants or flowers.

"Any ritual is an opportunity for transformation. To do a ritual, you must be willing to be transformed in some way. The inner willingness is what makes the ritual come alive and have power. If you aren't willing to be changed by the ritual, don't do it."

— STARHAWK

CHAPTER 10

Ceremony samples

I decided to offer many sample ceremonies to assist you in realizing how many ways that you can actually involve Ceremony in your daily life.

INVOKE THAT NEW "FEEL GOOD" JOB/CAREER

This could be done alone, or consider inviting friends who may be supportive of your new venture. You may write the key words to bring in on a piece of paper and place it in the sacred circle. A $1,000 increase in income, two weeks paid time off, working from home, using a specific talent, located in a specific town and pays for moving fees, etc.

"I call upon the blessings of The Supreme Being, Light and Love.

I call upon the Blessings of Mother Earth Gaia, the beautiful force that I come from. May you hear me, be with me and assist me on this endeavor today.

I Invoke your love and assistance, with (your goal). Allow the transition from one job to the next be smooth and with grace. Let me trust in this request and release all resistance to receiving the best for me. Show me clear signs along the way and open the doors to new places and people."

Assist this request to be in Ease and Humor.

Let this be in the highest good for everyone involved.

I ask now to receive a shift in my (career details you're asking for help in).

I receive your guidance, your wisdom, your love and your highest good for me. I am grateful for the shifting and letting go of (your shortcomings: scarcity, lack, settling, dissatisfaction, or unworthiness) whether I am aware or in denial of it.

I am grateful for the ease in ending (your current situation: i.e. current job, income that is unfulfilling). I am grateful to let go of all that has been in the way to my happy prosperity and sharing my talent. Thank you, Thank You, Thank you."

NEW RELATIONSHIP

"I call upon the blessings of The Supreme Being, Light and Love.

I call upon the Blessings of Mother Earth Gaia, the beautiful force that I come from. May you hear me, be with me and assist me on this endeavor today. I Invoke your love and assistance, with attracting and embracing a new relationship. I call in the relationship that is in alignment with my highest good. I lovingly allow myself to let go of all harmful and sabotaging beliefs from previous relationship experiences or ancestral beliefs. Please allow me to forgive myself and all others I have been in relationship with, so that I may move forward from a renewed place of gratitude and excitement. Let me receive a partner that is a comfortable match to me and I to them. Let us inspire each other and nurture each other in the ways we both need. Let us be harmonious but not boring. Please give me patience and discernment while I practice meeting people, trusting that I will know when I meet the right person. Assist me to feel at ease and truly loved before I meet this amazing person.

Assist this request to be in ease and understanding of (your desired goal).

Let this be in the highest good for everyone involved.

I ask to receive a loving relationship in alignment with my goal of (your goal), I ask to receive the next step and to clear signs along the way.

I receive your guidance, your wisdom, your love and your highest good for me. I am grateful for the shifting and letting go of (your limiting beliefs).

I am grateful for the ease in ending the old, unfulfilling types of relationships. Thank you, Thank You, Thank you."

INVOKING AND ALLOWING MORE MONEY

"I call upon the blessings of The Supreme Being, Light and Love.

I call upon the Blessings of Mother Earth Gaia, the beautiful force that I come from. May you hear me, be with me and assist me on this endeavor today. I Invoke your love and assistance, with attracting and receiving an increase in income and finances.

I call in the job and career that is in alignment with my highest good. I lovingly allow myself to let go of all harmful and sabotaging beliefs about my income. I lovingly dissolve the limits on my income or other abundance. Please allow me to forgive myself and money so that I may move forward from a renewed place of gratitude and excitement for this beneficial relationship. Let me receive the offers necessary to move up. Let me feel confident and sure of taking new directions, even if it is different than how I planned. Give me patience and flexibility with the process.

Let this be for the highest good for all involved. Assist me to feel at ease and truly loved about receiving this ongoing blessing.

Assist this request to be in ease and understanding.

Let this be in the highest good for everyone involved.

I ask to receive an increase in my income and bank balance that steadily climbs annually. (You can also specify an amount if desired.)

I receive your guidance, your wisdom, your love and your highest good for me. I am grateful for the shifting and letting go of all things in my way, like dissatisfaction, suffering, competition or pity (add your limiting beliefs).

I am grateful for the ease in ending financial *"limits, poverty and struggle". Thank you, Thank You, Thank you."

UPGRADING TO A NEW HOME

"I call upon the blessings of The Supreme Being, Light and Love.

I call upon the Blessings of Mother Earth Gaia, the beautiful force that I come from. May you hear me, be with me and assist me on this endeavor today. I Invoke your love and assistance, with attracting and securing a new home for myself. I call in the support needed and a home that is in alignment with my highest good.

I lovingly allow myself to let go of all harmful and sabotaging beliefs that limit my experience of acquiring a home. Please allow me to let go of this current home from a renewed place of gratitude for how it has been supporting me now, and fill me with the excitement of receiving my new home. Let me be easily directed to the sellers or landlords and for the process to be filled with ease and wonder. Let me be the right match for this new home and seller or landlord so that we may support each other. Please provide me with patience and discernment during the process. Fill me with the trust of receiving the right place at the right price. Assist me to feel at ease and truly blessed.

Assist this request to be in ease and understanding.

Let this be in the highest good for everyone involved.

I ask to receive a new home within my price range, and that is exactly what I need.

I receive your guidance, your wisdom, your love and your highest good for me. I am grateful for the shifting and letting go of (your limiting beliefs).

I am grateful for the ease in ending a cycle of unfulfilling homes. Thank you, Thank You, Thank you."

STARTING A NEW BUSINESS

"I call upon the blessings of The Supreme Being, Light and Love.

I call upon the Blessings of Mother Earth Gaia, the beautiful force that I come from. May you hear me, be with me and assist me on this endeavor today. I Invoke your love and assistance, with opening a new business of (the venture you desire). I call in the people and support that is in alignment with both the business and my highest good.

I lovingly allow myself to let go of all harmful and sabotaging beliefs from previous jobs or careers.

Please fill me with the renewed gratitude for my ideas and abilities. Open the doors and channels for this success to flow easily. Let me trust in receiving the clients and customers that are a match to me and my business and I to them. Let this business support the community it resides in and vice versa. I lovingly allow humor and fun to infuse this process. Please give me patience and discernment when needed. Support my needs for location, inventory, employees, and all areas of running a business.

Assist this request to be in ease and understanding.

Let this be in the highest good for everyone involved.

I ask to receive the successful transition and opening of a new business for me.

I receive your guidance, your wisdom, your love and your highest good for me. I am grateful for the shifting and letting go of (your limiting beliefs).

I am grateful for the ease in ending the patterns of old, unfulfilling types of work, jobs, or careers. Thank you, Thank You, Thank you."

GETTING A LOAN

"I call upon the blessings of The Supreme Being, Light and Love.

I call upon the Blessings of Mother Earth Gaia, the beautiful force that I come from. May you hear me, be with me and assist me on this endeavor today. I Invoke your love and assistance, with attracting and securing a new loan. (You can include the type of loan). I call in the loan that is in alignment with my highest good.

I lovingly allow myself to let go of all limiting or sabotaging beliefs from previous experiences or ancestral beliefs.

Please allow me to open to the ease in walking these financial corridors. Bring me to a place of gratitude for the lending institutions and the possibilities they give to me. Let me receive a loan that is a comfortable match to my needs. Fill me with the perspective of miracles for receiving a good rate and agreement in my favor. Please give me patience and gratitude for the persons writing and executing the loans. Assist me to feel at ease and truly loved before I acquire this amazing loan.

Assist this request to be in ease and understanding.

Let this be in the highest good for everyone involved.

I ask to receive a beneficial and affordable loan for (your dollar amount).

I receive your guidance, your wisdom, your love and your highest good for me. I am grateful for the shifting and letting go of dissatisfaction, frustration, limits, negativity.

I am grateful for the ease in ending the experience of being limited by loans or finances. Thank you, Thank You, Thank you."

INVOKING HELP FOR OTHERS IN NEED

HEALTH

"I call upon the blessings of The Supreme Being, Light and Love.

I call upon the Blessings of Mother Earth Gaia, the beautiful force that I come from. May you hear me, be with me and assist me on this endeavor today. I Invoke your love and assistance for (the person's name).

Let my intentions be for their highest good for all that are involved. I ask for the right answers to be given in a way that can be understood. I ask for the right people to show up and support the next step of healing needed at this time. Fill us all with gratitude for the process and the flexibility needed. Allow (the person) to forgive themselves and any others that they may need to in association with the healing process. Let them see this situation from a different perspective and the lesson being provided. Let (the person) move forward from a renewed place of gratitude. Please bring patience and a strong will where needed. Assist (the person) to let go of resistance for healing. Let all transformations happen at a rate (the person) can easily adjust to. Let all changes happen in true alignment with their souls path and mission. Help me, as the loving support for (the person's name) to trust in how this all transpires.

Assist this request to be in ease and understanding.

Let this be in the highest good for everyone involved.

Thank you for assisting (the person) in the healing of (their symptoms or condition).

I receive your guidance, your wisdom, your love and your highest good for me. I am grateful for the shifting and letting go of perfection, hopelessness, or suffering and to transform (the limiting beliefs or fears they are aware of).

I am grateful for the ease in ending any limiting physical or emotional issues. Thank you, Thank You, Thank you."

BLESS A LIFE TRANSITION

DEATH AND PASSING OVER

"I call upon the blessings of The Supreme Being, Light and Love.

I call upon the Blessings of Mother Earth Gaia, the beautiful force that we all come from. May you hear me, be with me and assist me on this endeavor today. I Invoke your love and assistance with the transition from life to death. Please bless this process for (the person's name) and for all those involved.

Let those of us here find gratitude for the life of (the person). Allow us to be in wonder and awe of the life process. We gratefully release (the person) into the loving arms of another world. We trust in the love that prevails there. We trust in the love that prevails here to hold us as we adjust. Bring us peace and ease in expressing our grief.

Let us trust that all is well. Hold the memories of (the person) dear in our hearts for easy access and celebration. Bless our tender hearts to feel in the true capacity we were designed for. Bring rest, bring a letting go, and bring celebration for the new.

Assist this request to be in ease and understanding.

Let this be in the highest good for everyone involved.

I ask to receive a loving transition for (the person's name) and the healthy adjustment for all loved ones.

I receive your guidance, your wisdom, your love and your highest good for me. I am grateful for the shifting and letting go of shock, suffering, melancholy, blame or pity.

I am grateful for the ease in letting (the person) go into the loving arms of Spirit. Thank you, Thank You, Thank you."

BLESS A LIFE TRANSITION

BIRTH

"I call upon the blessings of The Supreme Being, Light and Love.

I call upon the Blessings of Mother Earth Gaia, the beautiful force that we all come from. May you hear me, be with me and assist me on this endeavor today. I Invoke your love and assistance, with celebration of (the person's name). We are grateful to welcome this beautiful soul. Let us always be in wonder and awe of who they are as an individual.

May we support (the person) wholeheartedly. Let us be the best guides, teachers and students so that we can foster the highest good for (the person) and all those here today. I gratefully accept the responsibility to love and nurture this being to the best of my ability. Let me always see how I can be in alignment with what is truly needed. I am open to trusting what this child has to offer and that they will teach me much. I honor their wisdom and innocence in each situation. Bless their life with the people needed, the love of the planet, and the connection to Divinity. Assist them on the chosen soul path. We call in the nurturing mother energy to assist the parents to always know what to give and how much. Bless these parents to be the sustenance this child needs.

Assist this request to be in ease and understanding.

Let this be in the highest good for everyone involved.

I ask that we all honor the celebration of (the person's name).

We welcome you, (the person), to this Earth Plane.

May we receive guidance, your wisdom, your love and the

highest good for (the person) and all involved. I am grateful for the shifting and letting go of pregnancy and an ease in the mother's body to adjust to the nurturing of herself and (the person) in a different way now. We are grateful to release any limiting beliefs or feelings like uncertainty or fear.

We love you (the person's name).

Thank you, Thank You, Thank you."

BLESS A LIFE TRANSITION

MENOPAUSE

"I call upon the blessings of The Supreme Being, Light and Love.

I call upon the Blessings of Mother Earth Gaia, the beautiful force that we all come from. May you hear me, be with me and assist me on this endeavor today. I invoke your love and assistance with the transition from fertility to infertility, from Maiden to Crone. Please bless this beautiful life process for (the person's name).

Let those of us here find gratitude for how (the person) has lived her life. We receive her now as a wisdom keeper. Let us lovingly support her during this time in the way she needs. Let us trust her wisdom to help us as well.

Assist this request to be in ease and understanding.

Let this be in the highest good for everyone involved.

I ask to receive a loving transition for (the person's name) and the healthy adjustment for her body and mind. I ask that her loved ones are also touched by this graceful graduation.

I receive your guidance, your wisdom, your love and your highest good for (the person's name). Let her be grateful for the shifting and letting go of any negative limits like fear, shock, suffering, melancholy, anger or pity. Assist (the person) to let go of (her limiting beliefs).

I ask for the release of all ancestral patterns that may sabotage a healthy transition into the Wise Crone place in society.

I am grateful to be honoring (the person) as a wise Elder Woman. Welcome to our loving arms. Teach us and guide us now in the way only you can. Thank you, Thank You, Thank you."

BLESS A LIFE TRANSITION

MENARCHE

A girl's transition into Womanhood

"I call upon the blessings of The Supreme Being, Light and Love.

I call upon the Blessings of Mother Earth Gaia, the beautiful force that we all come from. May you hear me, be with me and assist me on this endeavor today. I Invoke your love and assistance, with the transition from Child to Maiden, from Child to Fertility. Please bless this beautiful life process for (the person's name).

Let those of us here find gratitude for how (the person) has grown and continues to mature in her life. We receive her now as a healthy, vibrant woman in our society. Let us lovingly support her during this time in the way she needs. Let us trust her wisdom to help us as well.

Assist this request to be in ease and understanding.

Let this be in the highest good for everyone involved.

I ask to receive a loving transition for (the person's name) and the healthy adjustment for her body and mind. I ask that her loved ones are also touched by this graceful graduation, and that they will support her in the way she needs to be supported. Let her feel the love of her community as we honor her in this new season.

Let (the person) receive your guidance, your wisdom, your love and your highest good. Let her be grateful for the shifting and letting go of any negative limits like fear, shock, suffering, *melancholy, anger or pity. Let her be supported by the older woman in her community to move gracefully into womanhood.*

I ask for the release of all ancestral patterns that may sabotage a healthy transition into this new season.

We are all grateful to be honoring (the person's name) as a Young Woman now. Welcome to our loving arms. Teach us and guide us in the way only you can. Thank you, Thank You, Thank you."

BLESS A LIFE TRANSITION

MARRIAGE

"I call upon the blessings of The Supreme Being, Light and Love.

I call upon the Blessings of Mother Earth Gaia, the beautiful force that we all come from. May you hear me, be with me and assist me on this endeavor today. I Invoke your love and assistance, with the Union of (one person's name) and (the other person's name).

Please continue to bless this beautiful life commitment to be full of grace, honor, abundance and freedom of self-expression.

Let those of us here Celebrate this Union. Let us support them in the way they most need. Let us also know when to be less involved. Let us trust their wisdom and ability to learn the ways of their relationship.

Let this be in the highest good for everyone involved.

I ask to receive a blessing for the hearts of all here today. That we are in alignment for the highest good to take place for (one person) and (the other person). We ask for the healthy adjustment to marriage and all the aspects of this type of intimate relationship for them.

Let them feel the love of their community and trust us to be their support in any situation. We honor this beautiful commitment they have for each other.

Let (one person's name) and (the other person's name) receive your guidance, your wisdom, your love and your blessings of the highest good.

Let us all be grateful for the shifting and letting go of previous negative beliefs or patterns that have affected family and societal relationships in an unbalanced way. Let us call in for them a new and improved version, a version with more purity of heart.

I am grateful to be honoring (one person) and (the other person) as a married couple, lovers and friends. Welcome into our loving arms. Teach us and guide us in the way only you can. Thank you, Thank You, Thank you."

Citations by Chapter

CHAPTER TWO:

1. Wikipedia contributors. "Magic Circle." *Wikipedia, The Free Encyclopedia*, https://en.wikipedia.org/w/index.php?title=Magic_circle&oldid=1143034107.

2. Regnier, R. (1994). "The Sacred Circle – a Process Pedagogy of Healing." *Interchange* vol. 25, pp. 129–144.

3. Gummer, Simon. (2013). "Circle Symbolism." *Simon Gummer OCA MA.* https://simongummerocama.wordpress.com/2013/07/14/circle-symbolism/.

4. Davidson, Sharmon. (2018). "Sacred Circles." *Sharmon Davidson Art.* https://sharmondavidson.com/sacred-circles/.

5. "Sacral Circle – Meaning and Symbolism." *Sacred Stories*. https://sacredstories.com/sacralcircleinfo/.

6. "Sacred Circles."

7. Bremner, Margaret. (2011). "Circle Symbolism." *Enthusiastic Artist.* https://enthusiasticartist.blogspot.com/2011/01/circle-symbolism.html.

CHAPTER FIVE:

8. "Prayer." *Dictionary.com*. https://www.dictionary.com/browse/prayer.

9. "Invocation." *Dictionary.com*. https://www.dictionary.com/browse/invocation.

CHAPTER NINE:

10. "Naysayer." *Merriam-Webster*. https://www.merriam-webster.com/dictionary/naysayer.